THE
ABORTION DEBATE

Claudia Caruana

THE MILLBROOK PRESS
Brookfield, Connecticut

Published by The Millbrook Press
2 Old New Milford Road
Brookfield, CT 06804
© 1992 Blackbirch Graphics, Inc.
First Edition
5 4 3 2 1

Created and produced in association with Blackbirch Graphics.
Series Editor: Bruce S. Glassman

Library of Congress Cataloging-in-Publication Data
Caruana, Claudia M.
    The abortion debate / by Claudia M. Caruana.
        p.   cm. — (Headliners)
    Includes bibliographical references and index.
    Summary: Examines historic and contemporary legal decisions regarding
abortion, on both the state and federal level.
    ISBN 1-56294-311-1   (lib. bdg.)
    1. Abortion—United States—Juvenile literature. 2. Abortion—Law and
legislation—United States—Juvenile literature. 3. Pro-choice movement—
United States—Juvenile literature. 4. Pro-life movement—United
States—Juvenile literature. [1. Abortion—Law and legislation.] I. Title.
II. Series.
HQ767.5.U5C378   1992
363.4'6—dc20   92-22417
                                                                CIP
                                                                AC

Editor's Note
Because of the complex nature of this topic, many editors had a
hand in the creation of this book. A significant portion of this
book was researched and developed by Tulin D. Faulkner, who
took great pains in helping us to present these issues in a
comprehensive and unbiased way.

Contents

Chapter 1

A Clash of Beliefs

Early one Saturday morning in April 1992, several women and girls enter the waiting room of a Planned Parenthood clinic. The clinic, like many other women's health centers across the country, offers a variety of services. Resident gynecologists—physicians who specialize in caring for female reproductive organs—perform annual checkups, prescribe birth-control pills and other contraceptive devices, test for cancer and sexually transmitted diseases, and administer the simple test that determines if a woman is pregnant. These clinics often treat herpes, gonorrhea, chlamydia, and other, more minor, infections. And for the past twenty years, the physicians at such clinics have been performing abortions.

An American Reality

The clinic has scheduled only abortion cases on this spring day. At the front entrance, a man and a woman hand out leaflets and talk about abortion to anyone who will listen. They follow women to the clinic door, talking rapid-fire about the sacredness of human life. They are "pro-life" advocates. They believe that abortion is a crime, no matter what reasons a woman or her physician might have for terminating a pregnancy.

The abortion debate focuses on our most deeply held values and the question of public law versus individual privacy.

Opposite:
Pro-life and pro-choice advocates face off at a demonstration in New York City.

The clinic staff calls the pro-life couple "our regulars." On some mornings other pro-life advocates join them. But these two protesters come faithfully twice a week, on the days the clinic sets aside for abortions. The clinic cannot have the pro-lifers arrested for approaching its patients. As long as they protest peacefully, without physically blocking a patient's way, the couple has a right to be there. The U.S. Constitution protects their freedom of speech and right to demonstrate peacefully.

The five patients in the waiting room know they also have a right to be at the clinic. Since 1973, women like them have had the legal right to decide whether or not to have an abortion. They sit quietly in chairs that have been arranged in a semicircle.

A thirteen-year-old girl who is ten weeks pregnant perches anxiously on the edge of her seat next to her mother. She had considered having the baby and then putting it up for adoption. But she decided that giving away her baby might haunt her for the rest of her life. Her parents worried about how carrying the pregnancy to term might affect her health. They had read that a very young girl's health was more endangered by full-term pregnancy than it was by an early abortion. Her parents also felt that pregnancy would disrupt her young life.

A young girl not much older than fifteen sits lost in her thoughts. Her best friend is with her. She is here because she became pregnant when she was raped. She knows that she wants to end her pregnancy.

Sitting alone next to the teenager is a woman in her twenties who became pregnant when her birth-control method failed. Already the single mother of two, she gets public assistance to take care of her children. She feels certain that she cannot support another child.

Across the room sits a woman over forty whose private physician referred her to the clinic. A genetic test revealed that the twelve-week-old fetus in her womb is developing abnormally. She feels that being a mother is a lifelong

A woman speaks with a counselor at a Planned Parenthood clinic. The clinic—like many others around the country— offers birth-control and abortion counseling as well as pregnancy-related medical care.

job; she feels sure that she won't have the stamina or the courage to be a good mother to a disabled child.

The fifth woman, in her early thirties, has come to the clinic twice before. She is here for her third abortion. She says there is no room in her life for children. Because she is already fourteen weeks pregnant, she will be referred somewhere else if she wants an abortion. This clinic provides abortions only between the eighth and twelfth week of pregnancy.

A counselor—a young woman with a master's degree in social work—comes out and calls the name of the first patient, the woman over forty. The counselor will discuss her medical history and the kind of birth control she uses and will ask the woman whether she is sure that abortion is the right choice for her. The pregnant woman feels reluctant at first to talk about her decision to have an abortion. So far, she has discussed it only with her husband and her physician. But the counselor is understanding, gentle, and nonjudgmental.

A Difficult Decision

Ending a pregnancy is something many women don't talk about publicly. Abortion is a difficult decision. It poses many personal and ethical questions. When can a fetus be considered a human life? At conception? In the sixth month of pregnancy? At birth? Is abortion okay when a woman's health would be harmed by continuing the pregnancy all the way to childbirth? What if the woman feels that she could not properly take care of the child? Is abortion justified when the pregnancy is the result of rape or incest? What if the fetus is diseased or deformed? Does a woman have the right to end a pregnancy to protect her way of life, her own well-being, or her family's well-being?

These are the kinds of emotional questions that women and their families ask themselves when faced with an unwanted pregnancy. For millions of Americans, these very questions have fueled one of the most heated public debates in the nation's recent history.

Pro-Life or Pro-Choice?

On a brisk Sunday morning—April 5, 1992—more than 500,000 men and women marched on Capitol Hill in Washington, D.C. Attending from all over the country, the crowd was "pro-choice." Mostly women and mostly under forty, they sang songs and shouted slogans that celebrated "reproductive freedom." They chose that moment in time to show their support for the "right to choose" abortion because the Supreme Court had begun hearings on a major abortion case, *Planned Parenthood of Southeastern Pennsylvania* v. *Casey.* Many who are pro-choice feared that the increasingly conservative Supreme Court was going to use this case to overturn its landmark 1973 decision, *Roe* v. *Wade,* in favor of stricter abortion controls.

The pro-choice demonstration was one of the largest in the nation's history. It was significantly larger than the

More than half a million pro-choice advocates converged in Washington, D.C., for a rally in April 1992. The demonstration was the largest in the nation's history.

pro-choice demonstration held in 1989, during the time that the Supreme Court was deliberating another major abortion case, *Webster* v. *Reproductive Health Services.* That rally had drawn more than 300,000 supporters. And in 1990, over 200,000 people had demonstrated against abortion rights.

Meanwhile, Operation Rescue—one of the country's most conservative and most active anti-abortion groups— was planning a different kind of demonstration in Buffalo, New York. Headed by the outspoken Randall Terry, the group spent two weeks in April 1992 blockading entrances to Buffalo abortion clinics, rallying in the streets, and trying to stop local women from getting abortions. The group's mission, to "rescue" the unborn, takes it all over the country, from Wichita, Kansas; to Washington, D.C.; to Baton Rouge, Louisiana.

The "rescuers" often get arrested for disorderly conduct or for preventing others from exercising their legal rights. Their graphic tactics, such as exhibiting a real twenty-week-old fetus they call "Baby Tia," also successfully shock many people.

The Pressure to Choose Sides

The controversy over abortion did not happen overnight. It has been brewing since the early 1960s. By the late 1960s, abortion-rights activists were rallying their cause on the streets and taking it into courts across the country. Both sides began to use the media—television, radio, newspapers, and magazines—to advertise, debate, and preach. Pro-life groups and individuals began blockading and even bombing abortion clinics in the 1970s. These acts of terrorism by pro-life groups caused great damage to medical facilities. The damage for the first nine months of 1992 alone was estimated at over $1.7 million.

Pressure from pro-life groups caused many physicians to stop performing abortions. Some physicians were harassed and threatened at their homes and at their clinics by anti-abortion groups. Other physicians stopped out of fear or simply because they did not like doing abortions.

Both pro-life and pro-choice groups formed powerful lobbies to petition state legislators and members of Congress to pass bills that would either restrict or ensure access to abortion. In 1973 alone, some 200 bills on abortion were introduced in state legislatures.

Politicians were soon compelled to choose sides in the abortion debate. They came to believe that their positions on abortion might carry as much weight at election time as their views on the economy and the environment. As sides were defined, the Republican party became anti-abortion; the Democrats stood largely for abortion rights.

"A Clash of Absolutes"

The central question of the abortion debate is often phrased as follows: "Which is a greater personal right, a pregnant woman's right to choose abortion, or a fetus's right to be born?" The answers offered by some pro-life and pro-choice advocates have been called "a clash of absolutes." Those who believe that a woman has an absolute right to decide the fate of her own body may never agree with those who believe that a fetus has the same right to life as a person who has already been born.

Normally, most Americans pride themselves on being a nation in which people with clashing beliefs can peacefully coexist. How, then, did these opposing beliefs about a personal and emotional issue become the subject of such a divisive public and legal dispute?

How this split happened is a complex story in itself, with many plot twists, themes, and major characters. The story began in back alleys of American cities, where people—not always doctors—performed often deadly illegal abortions. As a result of these tragic circumstances, many women demanded and gained more rights. The story's real climax took place in the chambers of the U.S. Supreme Court in 1973. An anonymous young woman who could not get a legal abortion in her home state of Texas took her case to the highest court in the country. On January 22, the nine justices of the Court declared a decision in that now-famous case, *Roe* v. *Wade*. What they decided set off two decades of bitter debate that would continue in full force to this day.

Two weeks after the giant 1992 pro-choice rally in Washington, D.C., pro-life forces stepped up their campaign to close down abortion clinics. Here, demonstrators huddle together in prayer as they block the entrance to a clinic in Buffalo, New York.

Abortion in America: A Brief History

There were no written abortion laws in colonial or eighteenth-century America. Under common law (unwritten law based on judicial cases), abortion was legal as long as it occurred before "quickening."

Quickening, the point in the pregnancy when a woman can feel the fetus moving (usually about the fifth month) was long considered the measure of when a fetus becomes a live human being. Little was known about the developing embryo. Without medical tests for pregnancy, quickening was sometimes the first clear sign that a woman was pregnant. Women have historically been unwilling to have an abortion after quickening. (Today, less than 1 percent of abortions occur after the fourth month of pregnancy, and virtually none occur after the sixth month.)

Abortion as Birth Control

In the nineteenth century, more and more American women began to use abortion to limit the size of their families. As more families left agriculture to work in urban industries, large families became less desirable. (Agricultural communities had favored large families because children could help on the farm.) In the second half of the century, large numbers of immigrant men and women also joined the urban work force. Unable to afford the time or the money to raise more children, many struggling immigrant women resorted to abortion. But native-born, affluent women were also increasingly using abortion to limit family size. During the course of the century, the birth rate among white American women dropped from 7.04 to 3.56 children.

Dangerous Methods

The first laws to limit abortions were passed in Connecticut in 1821, Missouri in 1825, and Illinois in 1827. They were intended only to protect women from an often lethal method of abortion—the use of poisons. The laws prohibited the use of "dangerous poisons" in an abortion, but even then only after quickening. Another wave of laws, in the 1840s, went after the abortionists who advertised and sold their dangerous drugs through popular magazines.

Concern over risky abortion methods led other states to pass restrictive laws through the first half of the nineteenth century. But these laws were rarely enforced. The public generally tolerated abortion, in part because the reproductive care of women was considered a private and domestic matter.

The Doctor Knows Best

The medical community launched the first organized attempt to restrict abortion. In 1847, trained physicians formed the American Medical Association (AMA) to professionalize their practice. Their original aim was to prevent anyone but physicians trained at established schools from practicing medicine. Abortionists were one of their major targets. But the physicians faced an unregulated and secretive abortion industry. Soon the more radical members of the AMA pushed for a major campaign to criminalize abortion.

Led by Dr. Horatio Storer, an obstetrician and gynecologist, the AMA launched media and lobbying campaigns to persuade the public that abortion was a crime and to promote stricter state legislation against abortion. The fetus's right to life became an issue for the first time. Dr. Storer and his followers also argued that abortion must be stopped because of the high rate of abortion among white Protestant women, a trend they called "race suicide."

A doctor examines his patient in the late 1800s.

Strict Laws

The AMA campaign was effective. By 1880, forty states had passed laws that made abortion a criminal act at any stage of pregnancy. However, most of the laws would permit abortion if a physician believed that it was necessary in order to save the woman's life. Meanwhile, the do-it-yourself abortion industry was targeted by the Comstock Laws of 1873, which prohibited the mail-order sale of abortifacients (instruments and drugs used to induce abortion). Ironically, the Comstock Laws also forbade the mailing of contraceptives. The lack of birth-control methods would be a major reason for the high rate of abortions until the mid-twentieth century.

Safer Methods

Two important medical innovations in the late 1800s helped to reduce the dangers of abortion. In 1879, Helgar dilators were invented. These were metal rods that dilated the opening of the cervix (entrance to the uterus) so that instruments could be inserted to remove the embryo or fetus. Previously, many women had bled to death because instruments were inserted by puncturing the cervix and uterus. Also, antiseptic (sterile) methods began to be used in both childbirth and abortions during the 1890s. This helped reduce the number of deaths from poisoning.

Strict abortion laws and medical advances did little to end the rate of illegal and dangerous abortions in the twentieth century. In 1936, at the height of the Depression (a decade when many Americans were poor and unemployed), more than 500,000 illegal abortions were being performed in the United States every year.

Living with the Law

By the 1950s, physicians began to feel the burden of the strict abortion laws they had helped to create a century before. Abortion techniques were much safer than they had been. Also, physicians were often torn between the desperation of a patient who wanted an abortion and the law, which permitted abortion only to "save the life of the mother." They began to seek exceptions for patients who had been raped, for example, or whose health—but not life—might be endangered by the pregnancy. Hospitals, where all legal abortions were performed, responded to the physicians' dilemma by setting up abortion committees that helped decide whether an abortion could be performed.

A Time for Reform

The first important step toward liberalizing nineteenth-century abortion laws came from the legal profession. In 1959, the American Law Institute proposed that abortion should be legal if the pregnancy would "gravely impair the physical or mental health of the mother," or if the child would be born "with grave physical or mental defects," and when the pregnancy resulted from rape or incest.

A decade later, fourteen states had passed laws modeled after the Law Institute's proposal. The support for reformed abortion laws had grown to include physicians, women's-rights groups, several religious groups, and the public. The public reacted especially strongly to the tragic stories of women who had been unable to get legal abortions for birth defects.

The major opposition to abortion rights throughout the 1960s came from the Catholic Church. Catholic clergymen had opposed abortion and birth control for centuries. But now they began political lobbies to prevent liberal abortion laws. For the time being, state legislatures largely ignored the Catholic lobby on the grounds that the U.S. legal system recognized the separation of church and state.

An Issue for the Supreme Court

By 1973, when the U.S. Supreme Court was ready to announce its decision in *Roe* v. *Wade*, several major court cases had been won against "vague" state abortion laws and for the "right to privacy" in sexual matters. The Court weighed these precedents in its decision. It also considered public support and the more liberal attitudes toward sexuality in the 1960s.

The justices also looked at the legal history of abortion. They noted that the century-old abortion laws effective in most states had come about because of the high risk of nineteenth-century abortion methods. Antiseptic procedures, antibiotics, dilators, and—more recently—the vacuum aspiration method had made an early abortion less of a health risk than childbirth by 1973. The main legal reason for restricting abortion rights, the justices argued, no longer existed. The legal system, they added, should not pass moral judgments on abortion.

EQUAL·JUSTICE·UNDER·LAW

14

Chapter 2

The *Roe* v. *Wade* Landmark

Roe v. *Wade*, the Texas lawsuit that changed the legal status of abortion in America, was the brainchild of two young women lawyers, Linda Coffee and Sarah Weddington. In 1969, Coffee and Weddington had only recently graduated from the University of Texas Law School. Although 1969 was not long ago, women were only beginning to enter the legal profession during this time. Coffee and Weddington had performed well at school and had expected the same doors to open for them as had for the bright and talented men who graduated with them. But they were soon disappointed.

Closed Doors for Women

Most powerful law firms during the 1960s weren't interested in hiring women. To build up her résumé, Linda Coffee spent a year as a law clerk in the fifth circuit of the federal court system. When she went out again to look for a well-paying corporate job, she ended up with only one offer. A smaller law firm that needed a young lawyer hired her at a modest salary to practice bankruptcy law—something few young lawyers wanted to do in the late 1960s.

Sarah Weddington had an even harder time finding the corporate law job that she felt she deserved. Finally, she decided to bide her time by working for a law professor.

The 1973 Supreme Court decision drastically changed the status of abortion in America.

Opposite:
The Supreme Court in Washington, D.C., is the ultimate battleground for both sides of the abortion issue.

Lawyer Sarah Weddington became interested in the legal issues surrounding women's reproductive rights in the 1960s. Her involvement led her to pursue a case that eventually became the landmark *Roe v. Wade*.

Weddington's work at least gave her time to notice what was happening in America. Perhaps because of her own personal experience, her attention soon focused on the feminist movement, which had been building momentum for the better part of the decade.

Women involved in the feminist movement in the 1960s were generally considered "radicals"—extremists who wanted to upset the time-honored traditions of American society. An aspiring young lawyer in a conservative state like Texas seriously risked her career by supporting feminism openly. But Weddington had no corporate boss to please. She joined a feminist group, the National Organization for Women (NOW) and became active in Planned Parenthood, the national birth-control organization. She also worked to get women to run for public office.

Weddington eagerly volunteered her legal expertise to a "pregnancy counseling service." The service provided women who wanted abortions with the names of doctors who were known to provide safe and affordable—albeit illegal—abortions. Modeled after the Clergy Consultation Service (CCS) on Abortion, which was created by Protestant and Jewish clergymen in 1967, such services were set up by volunteer groups across the country.

Weddington's job was to make sure the counseling service stayed out of legal trouble; helping a woman to get an illegal abortion was punishable by law in Texas. But this part of the abortion law was rarely enforced. Besides, as long as the group merely *informed* women but did not *arrange* the abortions, they felt they were still within the law. But Weddington soon realized that she wanted to do something about the abortion laws themselves.

Reality and the Law

Because of her work at the pregnancy counseling service, Weddington became aware of the serious conflict between abortion laws and what many women actually did when faced with an unwanted pregnancy. In the 1960s, there was no federal law on abortion. Abortion laws were set state by state, and many states were strict.

Texas, with one of the strictest laws, allowed abortion only if the woman's life was threatened by the pregnancy. Anyone who performed an abortion or helped a woman obtain an abortion could legally be prosecuted. Unchanged since 1859, the Texas abortion statute was also among the oldest in the country.

Most states had reformed their abortion laws by the late 1960s. New laws included at least a few other grounds for legal abortion. The most common additional grounds were pregnancies resulting from rape or incest, evidence that a fetus was seriously deformed, and a physician's conclusion that a pregnancy would impair a woman's physical or mental health.

In reality, the laws succeeded in limiting only *legal* abortions. At the time, eight to ten thousand legal abortions were reported every year. According to certain Planned Parenthood estimates, anywhere from a million to a million-and-a-half abortions took place illegally each year in the late 1960s. Critics of restrictive abortion laws wondered whom the laws were serving if so many women were breaking the law to obtain needed abortions.

A Necessary Crime?

Weddington, like many other women by the late 1960s, viewed abortion as a women's issue that was tied to winning equality for women in society. She felt that women had to gain complete control of their own reproductive capabilities before they could be as free as men. Access to abortion was one way to ensure that control.

From Weddington's point of view, the abortion laws—even the reformed laws in other states—took a woman's control of her own body away and gave it to the state and to physicians. Many women desperately needed that control; they needed to decide when and where they would bear children. In order to have that control, many women were willing to resort to illegal abortions.

Weddington thought that reforming Texas's laws to include more reasons for legal abortion was not enough. Reformed laws still left the decision and the responsibility for the abortion up to a physician. Many women found it easier—and less humiliating—to end a pregnancy secretly than to convince an authority figure (usually a man) that they were victims of rape or incest, for example.

Another common argument against existing abortion laws was that they discriminated against poor women. Laws that allowed abortion when a woman's mental health was in danger were vague enough to cover a number of personal reasons that women chose abortion. But this, too, required an outside judgment by a sympathetic family doctor. Critics argued that middle-class and more affluent women were more likely to get sympathetic treatment because they tended to be under the regular care of a private doctor. The poor, it was pointed out, rarely had the luxury of regular medical care. They generally went to a doctor—often at an impersonal public clinic—only when they had a medical emergency. Also, upper- and middle-class women were more likely to be able to afford the private fees and hospital costs of a legal abortion. The poor, it was argued, scrambled to raise the cash needed for an illegal abortionist's one-time fee.

In the 1960s, as now, many women who sought abortions were young and single and were suddenly faced with unplanned pregnancies. Although in reality more and more people were sexually active outside of marriage in the 1960s, social attitudes toward pregnancy out of wedlock were still severe. Single mothers and their children faced varying degrees of social disapproval. The existing laws exposed single young women who sought legal abortions to shame and rejection. Also, the "acceptable" reasons for abortion generally did not apply to them.

Fetal deformity, for example, was a relatively limited problem that concerned married, and often older, women with planned pregnancies. Pregnancies caused by rape or incest were tragic, but they made up a small percentage of unwanted pregnancies. Single young women, then, often chose the privacy of illegal abortions. Secret abortions protected them from the scorn of their families, physicians, and hospital boards.

A Risky Option

Illegal abortions were secretive, "back alley" operations. Although even illegal abortion procedures were relatively safe by the late 1960s, there was no way to monitor the skills and methods of underground abortionists.

Some licensed physicians performed illegal abortions after hours, but persons with limited medical training were also in the abortion business. The place where an illegal abortion was performed could be relatively sanitary, with sterilized equipment, carefully administered anesthesia (drugs that numb pain), and a supply of antibiotics (drugs to treat infections). Then again, many women reported getting abortions on dirty kitchen tables, without anesthesia, or with crude implements. Women who sought illegal abortions ran the risk of fatal blood contaminations caused by unsterilized surgical equipment, ruptures caused by careless or hurried operations, and the complications of half-finished abortions. Newspaper accounts of botched abortions, maimings, and even deaths often revealed the victims to be poor, very young, or both.

Beginnings of a Court Case

Sarah Weddington found an ally against Texas's abortion laws in Linda Coffee. The two women began to talk often and realized that both of them saw abortion as a women's-rights issue. To them, the abortion situation in America was both a legal and a social problem.

Linda Coffee, a Dallas lawyer, joined forces with Sarah Weddington in 1969. Together, they built a case that was the first to challenge strict abortion laws in the United States.

Social equality for women had become a cause for both lawyers as well. Coffee was also disillusioned by the meager rewards that the legal establishment offered to women lawyers. She called herself the only "feminist lawyer" in Dallas. Like Weddington, she joined NOW and became active in women's rights. Both women were ambitious and eager to prove themselves as lawyers, and both were interested in working for social change.

The two lawyers began to talk more and more about abortion. Wouldn't a woman's right in so personal a matter be guaranteed by the Constitution? Could they create a test case against Texas's abortion laws? Even more dramatic, could they challenge the strict Texas law as unconstitutional?

Coffee's year as a law clerk in a federal court proved to be valuable experience that helped them to know exactly how to approach the court most effectively with an issue. Weddington's experience in abortion counseling had given her the background they needed to build a case.

Finding Plaintiffs

In 1969, Coffee and Weddington began to construct their case. What they needed was a plaintiff—someone who had a valid complaint against the Texas abortion laws. They interviewed several women, but none wanted to go through the rigors and possible embarrassment of a long court case. Then they met Norma McCorvey.

McCorvey was poor, single, and pregnant. She wanted an abortion but was told that she could not obtain one legally in Texas. She could not afford to travel to another state or country for the procedure, and she was afraid to have an illegal abortion. McCorvey agreed to be the plaintiff in the case but did not want her real name used. To protect her privacy, Coffee and Weddington named her "Jane Roe" in the lawsuit. (McCorvey herself would reveal her name to the public some ten years later.)

Meanwhile, the two lawyers had spoken with a young married couple also willing to be plaintiffs in the court case. Like McCorvey, the couple chose to remain anonymous and were called the "Does." Mrs. "Doe" was not pregnant, but the couple believed that if she ever did become pregnant she should have the option of terminating the pregnancy legally if she wished. The Does would not be strong plaintiffs because their complaint was only theoretical. But Coffee and Weddington decided to file them as plaintiffs anyway. The lawyers wanted to attack the state law from as many angles as possible. They felt that questioning a married couple's rights—in addition to those of Norma McCorvey—would lend some respectability to the case as a whole. McCorvey was, after all, a single, pregnant woman—something of a social stigma.

Another plaintiff joined the lawsuit after it had begun. James Hallford, a Dallas physician, had been indicted by the district attorney's office on two counts of performing illegal abortions. The physician's attorneys had been arguing that Hallford could not be indicted because the state's laws were vague and therefore unconstitutional. The last article of the Texas law permitted abortion "by medical advice for the purpose of saving the life of the mother." How could Dr. Hallford know, the lawyers had argued, if he was violating other articles of the statute if he was performing an abortion that, in his medical opinion, would save the mother's life?

Then Hallford's attorneys heard about the cases of Roe and Doe, which focused on the constitutional rights of individuals, rather than on technicalities in the statutes. They asked that Hallford's case be added to theirs. The judge in charge of the case agreed to merge the physician's case with Jane Roe's.

On March 16, 1970, Henry Wade, district attorney for Dallas, was sued by plaintiffs Jane Roe and John and Mary Doe. Dr. James Hallford was added as a plaintiff before the hearings began two months later.

Norma McCorvey agreed to be the plaintiff in Weddington and Coffee's Texas abortion case. To protect her privacy, McCorvey was given the name "Jane Roe" in the suit.

The Legal Question of Choice

Coffee and Weddington had worked hard for several months to research and prepare their cases for Jane Roe and the Does. The U.S. legal system relies heavily on precedents, or earlier court decisions that support the argument in a current case. So Coffee and Weddington spent a lot of time researching precedents. They found that there had been no previous court cases suing for a woman's right to choose abortion. The woman's right to choose for herself was central to the argument that Coffee and Weddington wanted to pursue. They soon discovered that theirs was a revolutionary argument.

In most abortion laws current in the late 1960s, there were two decision makers who had the authority to decide if an abortion could be performed: the state and qualified physicians. The woman's choice or desire was legally unimportant, and she usually could not be prosecuted.

State governments saw the legal protection of a person's life as the states's constitutional obligation. In the strictest laws, the life of a fetus was as important as a woman's, unless the fetus's life was endangering hers. The laws became necessarily vague about when a woman's life—or physical or mental health—was in danger. Lawmakers reasoned that these distinctions required medical expertise. Physicians were the most qualified to make decisions about health risks. And medical science had advanced greatly in the 1960s. But without clear guidelines about what constituted a risk to life or health, many physicians made decisions that required ethical authority as well as medical knowledge. This is where Coffee and Weddington thought the laws were seriously flawed. Does a physician or a state have greater ethical authority than the woman seeking the abortion? They thought not.

Although Coffee and Weddington wanted to preserve a woman's access to informed medical advice, they also wanted to make sure that the woman's decision was the final and most powerful one. They argued that most abortion questions required people to weigh conflicting interests. When was a health risk great enough to justify abortion? Was a potential, rather than actual, risk to a woman's life reason enough for an abortion? Would a pregnancy caused by rape or incest seriously affect a woman's mental health? Would the birth of a deformed baby affect a woman's physical and emotional well-being? Coffee and Weddington maintained that only the pregnant woman could best answer these personal questions.

The Precedents

Coffee and Weddington found a constitutional basis for a woman's right to choose in what was called the "due process clause" in the Fourteenth Amendment. According to this clause, no state is to enact a law depriving anyone of life, liberty, or property, without due process of law; nor is any state to deny to any person within its jurisdiction the equal protection of the laws. The two lawyers argued that Texas deprived women of liberty by denying their right to choose abortion without due process (a legal hearing). Three legal precedents helped the lawyers to develop this argument.

In 1961, the U.S. Supreme Court had heard *Griswold* v. *Connecticut*, which challenged an old Connecticut statute forbidding the sale of birth-control devices. The law, in effect, also prohibited the use of all forms of birth control. The Supreme Court decided that a married couple's right to purchase and use birth control was protected by a "zone of privacy" that was granted by several constitutional amendments, including the First and Fourteenth amendments.

The second precedent that would help the lawyers' argument was established in *People* v. *Belous*. It was a California Supreme Court case involving the arrest of a physician who had referred a couple to an abortionist.

The decision in the case was important to Coffee and Weddington for two reasons. First, the judges declared that California's abortion laws were vague and therefore violated the due process clause of the Fourteenth Amendment. The same argument would be used against Texas's laws in *Roe* v. *Wade*. Second, the judges declared that a woman's right to life should come before a state's interests in the unborn.

The third precedent-setting case that Weddington and Coffee would use was *United States* v. *Vuitch*. This 1969 lawsuit involved a doctor who was performing abortions in the nation's capital. Dr. Vuitch had been freely interpreting a Washington, D.C., law that permitted abortions to preserve a woman's life. He had performed "therapeutic" abortions. These were abortions of pregnancies that were not life threatening. Vuitch's case was heard in a federal district court. The court overturned Washington's existing abortion law, declaring it too vague to "guide either the doctor, the jury, or the Court."

The federal court system had historically stayed out of abortion law, and state courts had come to view abortion as an issue of "state interests." By overturning an abortion law in federal court, the district court in Washington had set a precedent for other federal courts to overturn state abortion laws.

The District Court Hearing

On May 22, 1970, Weddington and Coffee presented *Roe et al.* v. *Wade* in a court of appeals for the fifth district to argue against Henry Wade, the district attorney. Dr. Hallford's attorneys, Fred Bruner and Roy Merrill, also arrived with a detailed argument for their client.

Roe, the Does, and Hallford were filing what is called a "class-action" suit. That meant that each plaintiff suing the state also represented other people in the same "class," and the court's decision in Jane Roe's case would also apply to other single pregnant women seeking an abortion.

How the Supreme Court Works

How does the United States ensure that it can survive as a strong and orderly society, while at the same time protecting the individual rights of its citizens?

The key, Americans have come to believe, is a balanced constitution. The U.S. Constitution was intended to balance society's need for order with the individual's right to freedom. Three independent and equal branches of government—Congress, the Supreme Court, and the Presidency—are charged with making sure that the Constitution is honored.

The Supreme Court is the highest court in the United States. It handles a select number of unique and controversial cases each year. The nine justices, who are politically appointed rather than elected, do not actually hear the more than 5,000 civil and criminal cases that are filed in the Supreme Court each year. Most cases come from state and federal courts, but the Supreme Court has "original jurisdiction" in disputes between states or between a state and the federal government. The justices write opinions on approximately 250 to 280 cases per term. (A term runs from the first week of October to the last week of June.) "Plenary review," with oral arguments by attorneys, is usually granted to no more than 180 cases per term. Formal written opinions are delivered in 130 to 150 cases.

When the Supreme Court rules on a constitutional issue, its judgment cannot be overridden by any other court. The decision, however, can be overruled in two ways: a new constitutional amendment can be passed, or a new judgment can be made in a subsequent Supreme Court case to overrule the earlier judgment. Constitutional amendments are rare and difficult to pass. The Supreme Court, though, has overruled its own decisions more than a hundred times in its history.

Statues of Justice adorn the Supreme Court Building.

Roe and Mrs. Doe, their attorneys stated, had a constitutional right to choose an abortion. The abortion right was rooted in their right to privacy, life, and liberty. These rights, they argued, were protected by the Ninth and Fourteenth amendments of the Constitution. "Privacy" and "abortion" were not specifically named rights in the Constitution. But the Ninth Amendment could be interpreted as protecting "certain rights" even if they were not specifically spelled out. The Texas state abortion laws violated women's constitutional rights of privacy, liberty, and the right to choose what happens to their own bodies, Weddington and Coffee argued. On behalf of Roe and the Does, they asked the court to declare the Texas statutes unconstitutional. They also asked the court for "injunctive relief" from the Texas laws. In nonlegal language, injunctive relief meant that Jane Roe could get a legal abortion in Texas because the state would not be able to enforce the law.

The District Court Decision

The three judges for the fifth circuit made their decision on *Roe et al.* v. *Wade* in less than a month. They dismissed the Texas abortion laws as vague. They declared that the laws infringed on the constitutional rights of Jane Roe and James Hallford and members of their class. They dismissed the Does' case, saying that since Mrs. Doe was not pregnant, they did not have a legitimate complaint. The court would not grant injunctive relief.

The fifth-circuit decision sounded like a victory for Coffee and Weddington. But without injunctive relief, the decision simply meant that they had succeeded in testing the law, not changing it.

The lawyers decided to appeal the district court's decision. In 1971, Weddington and Coffee filed the case of *Roe* v. *Wade* with the U.S. Supreme Court. The Court had not yet accepted an abortion case. But Weddington and Coffee knew the time was now right to present one.

A Decade of Change

Weddington and Coffee were challenging abortion laws at a time when many people were working for social reform. The 1960s was a decade of many profound social changes, particularly in civil rights. Laws that limited the rights of blacks and of women had been challenged and overturned in court cases across the nation. The Civil Rights Act was passed in 1964, and segregation in schools was successfully contested in 1967. The federal courts were filled with challenges to outmoded laws.

A number of federal and state courts were hearing abortion-rights cases. Advocates of abortion-law reform had organized influential groups. The Association for the Study of Abortion had been in existence since 1964. In 1969, the pro-choice National Association for the Repeal of Abortion Laws was formed. Grass-roots groups worked to build community support for new, less-restrictive abortion laws. Even Planned Parenthood, which for several decades had avoided advocating abortion as a method of birth control, finally openly supported the nationwide repeal of abortion laws in 1969.

Public support for the repeal of restrictive abortion laws became widespread after two well-publicized events. The first concerned a twenty-nine-year-old mother of four named Shari Finkbine. In 1962, Finkbine was pregnant with her fifth child when she learned that Thalidomide, a prescription sedative she was taking, caused birth defects. Abortion was illegal in Arizona, Finkbine's home state, but Finkbine's physician had agreed to perform an abortion in the hospital—on the condition that Finkbine not tell anyone.

Although abortion was illegal in Arizona except to save the life of the mother, there were physicians who would bend the rules for "special cases." Such cases, however, had to be approved by the hospital's board of directors or a similar governing body.

Finkbine's legal problems began when her name was disclosed by the press. To help warn other women who might be taking Thalidomide, Finkbine had told a journalist friend about her own experience with the drug. Her story was published, and even though she had requested complete anonymity, the press soon discovered her name. People opposed to abortion responded with anger. Fearing bad publicity, the hospital refused Finkbine's request to terminate the pregnancy. Finkbine lost her job as the star of a children's show on television. Her husband was asked to take a leave of absence from his teaching job. The family received harassing letters and telephone calls and eventually had to receive protection from the FBI.

Shari Finkbine gained national attention when she struggled to obtain an illegal abortion in Arizona. Finkbine wanted to end her pregnancy because she had unwittingly taken a drug that was known to cause severe birth defects.

Finkbine took her case to court, but the judge upheld the Arizona law that banned abortion. It was decided that Finkbine's life was not in danger. Finally, in the twelfth week of her pregnancy, Finkbine went to Sweden to obtain an abortion. The fetus, it turned out, was severely deformed.

Finkbine's story gained much national and international attention. Many people were sympathetic to her situation. A national public opinion poll revealed that a majority of Americans believed that Finkbine should have had the legal right to terminate the pregnancy.

Another tragic event that swayed public opinion in favor of abortion rights was an epidemic of rubella, or German measles, between 1962 and 1965. Rubella was known to cause birth defects when contracted during pregnancy. If a woman had rubella during early pregnancy, potential birth defects could include deafness, blindness, and severe mental retardation. Many pregnant women who had rubella asked for abortions. Although restrictive abortion laws inhibited most doctors, some physicians privately performed the procedure, feeling that in such cases abortion was more merciful than allowing a severely impaired child to be born into a life of suffering.

Some fifteen thousand babies were born with birth defects as a result of the rubella epidemic. Such statistics led many physicians to seek abortion reform. In 1967, the American Medical Association declared that it favored more liberal abortion laws. By 1970, when *Roe* v. *Wade* was being prepared for the Supreme Court, the AMA favored abortion limited only by sound medical judgment.

Four states responded to the growing reform movement by repealing their strict abortion laws. In 1970, Hawaii, California, New York, and Washington eased most restrictions on early abortions.

A significant political event in the movement toward abortion reform was the support given to abortion rights by President Lyndon B. Johnson's administration. The executive branch of government had traditionally stayed out of the abortion debate, but the Johnson administration had appointed an advisory council on the status of women. In 1968, the council published a report that called for the repeal of all abortion laws. By 1971, the country seemed poised on the brink of reform; federal courts and the White House had paved the way for a Supreme Court decision on the abortion issue.

Roe v. *Wade* in Washington

The U.S. Supreme Court did decide to hear *Roe* v. *Wade*, but preparing the case would cost Weddington and Coffee a lot of work, time, and money. Texas fund-raisers helped them to pay for the work.

Weddington and Coffee received briefs from more than forty organizations and individuals who were in favor of liberalizing America's abortion laws. These "friends of the court," as they are called, included the attorney generals of several states, lawyers from women's groups, Planned Parenthood of America, the American College of Obstetricians and Gynecologists, and others. Weddington and Coffee used the valuable information that these "friends" provided to support their case.

Jane Roe et al. Appellant v. *Henry Wade* was argued in the Supreme Court in December 1971. On the same day, the Court heard another abortion case, *Doe* v. *Bolton*, which challenged Georgia's strict abortion laws.

Once the cases had been heard, the wait began for the Supreme Court's deliberations. But the wait was longer than most people had anticipated. The Supreme Court had a heavy caseload, and these abortion cases took a great deal of research and thought. It was also suspected that the abortion cases had set off a "political" debate among the justices. In the end, the justices put off *Roe* v. *Wade* and *Doe* v. *Bolton* until the next Supreme Court session. Both cases were reargued on October 11, 1972, nearly a year later.

Justice Harry A. Blackmun provided the majority opinion in *Roe* v. *Wade*. In the decision, Blackmun wrote—among many other things—that a state cannot interfere with a woman's decision to have an abortion in the first six months of pregnancy, except to protect the woman's health.

The Decision Comes Down

Many people were not aware that legal history was made on the day when *Roe* v. *Wade* and *Doe* v. *Bolton* were finally decided. It was January 22, 1973, and the death of former president Lyndon B. Johnson dominated the front pages of most newspapers. But it did not take long for the Supreme Court decision about an unmarried pregnant Texas woman to make national headlines.

Voting 7-2, the Supreme Court decided in favor of Jane Roe. It was a decision that surprised even those who had fought for abortion rights. A small test case prepared by two relatively inexperienced women attorneys had led to a landmark decision that overturned laws in forty-six states and had far-reaching effects on American society.

Justice Harry A. Blackmun, who wrote the Court's decision, declared the Texas abortion laws to be unconstitutional and noted the following:

- The right to privacy includes a woman's right to decide whether or not to have children. The right to privacy, and, therefore, the right to abortion, is protected by the Ninth and Fourteenth amendments.
- The state may have a right to regulate how abortions are performed for the woman's protection.
- The state may have an interest in protecting the life of the fetus after it reaches viability—a stage when it can survive outside the mother's body (usually set between twenty-four and twenty-eight weeks of pregnancy).
- During the first three months of pregnancy (first trimester), the woman can have an abortion without interference. The state can only insist that she consult with a physician. During the second trimester (the fourth through sixth months), the state can only impose restrictions to protect the woman's health.
- When the fetus is viable—that is, the last three months of pregnancy—the state can prohibit abortion, except when the mother's life or health is in danger.

Chapter 3

The Legal Aftershocks

Decades of debate and divisiveness followed the *Roe* v. *Wade* decision.

The Supreme Court's 1973 decision in *Roe* v. *Wade* surprised those who supported abortion rights as much as it upset anti-abortionists. The Court had not only declared most states' abortion laws to be unconstitutional, but it had also set up a system of guidelines that gave women the right to have an abortion—for whatever reason—in the first six months of pregnancy.

The reaction to such dramatic news was immediate and widespread. Women's-rights groups hailed the Supreme Court's decision as a major step forward in the battle to gain equal rights for women. The medical establishment welcomed the ruling for opening the way to long-overdue reform. The decision also had general public support. Polls at the time showed that 64 percent of the American public believed that the decision to have an abortion should be left up to a woman and her physician.

Abortion After 1973

Over 760,000 legal abortions were performed in 1973. The rate of legal abortions rose steadily until 1980 and then leveled off. Illegal-abortion rates dropped dramatically, from over a million a year to several thousand.

One advantage gained by women seeking legal abortions after 1973 was access to affordable, safe abortions

Opposite:
In the years that followed *Roe* v. *Wade*, both pro-life and pro-choice forces improved their organization and intensified their efforts to fight their opposition.

outside hospitals. In *Doe* v. *Bolton*, the companion case to *Roe* v. *Wade*, the Supreme Court had decided that an abortion does not have to be performed in a hospital. Only a licensed physician was required. Groups like Planned Parenthood and the National Abortion Rights Action League (NARAL) quickly mobilized to help set up private clinics across the country. The clinics offered abortions that were more affordable than those in hospitals, as well as other services, such as counseling and birth-control materials. By 1980, the majority of abortions were performed in private clinics rather than in hospitals.

Why Women Had Abortions

With legalized abortion came accurate record-keeping. For the first time, it was possible to know who had abortions and why. Agencies and research groups like the Centers for Disease Control and the Alan Guttmacher Institute (AGI) began to conduct surveys of clinics and health departments. A 1987 survey by AGI found that

Faye Wattleton was president of Planned Parenthood from 1978 to 1992. During the years after the *Roe* v. *Wade* decision, groups such as the National Abortion Rights Action League (NARAL) and Planned Parenthood worked to set up clinics across the country to provide access to safe, legal abortions.

most women have three to four reasons for seeking an abortion. The following reasons were given most often:

- A baby would disrupt work, schooling, or other responsibilities.
- Can't afford a baby right now.
- Do not have a strong relationship with the father and want to avoid single parenthood.
- Unready for the responsibility of motherhood.

A far smaller number of women reported that they wanted an abortion because of possible fetal defects, health problems, rape, or incest.

Who Had Abortions

The Guttmacher Institute also found that women of all races and income levels were having abortions. The survey showed these trends:

- In absolute numbers, white, single women between the ages of eighteen and twenty-five had the most abortions.
- In proportion to their total population, African-American and Hispanic women were more likely to have abortions than white women.
- Proportionately more women with family incomes below $11,000 a year had abortions than middle-class women.
- The groups most likely to choose abortion over childbirth were teens aged fifteen and under and women who were forty and over.

Roe v. *Wade* had succeeded in making abortion a safe, medically supervised procedure. But the decision also fueled a growing debate about abortion rights.

Hate Mail and Accusations

The Supreme Court, which routinely passes down judgments with little public comment, was astonished when it received over 40,000 pieces of mail on its *Roe* v. *Wade* decision. The fact that hate mail arrived as often as congratulations was a sign of just how divisive the abortion debate was in America.

The two justices who had voted against the majority decision in *Roe* v. *Wade*, William Rehnquist and Byron White, believed that the Supreme Court was abusing its power. They stated that the Court should not impose a constitutional barrier in "a sensitive area such as this."

Many people agreed with Rehnquist and White. Many individuals who opposed abortion rights felt that the decision violated a deep-seated belief among many Americans that abortion was wrong.

The Supreme Court decision raised questions that are still hotly debated to this day. Most of those questions have revolved around three concepts in that decision: personhood, viability, and states' rights.

William Rehnquist was one of two justices who opposed the *Roe* v. *Wade* decision. In 1986, Rehnquist was appointed chief justice by President Ronald Reagan.

"Personhood"

When the Supreme Court decided that a pregnant woman had rights protected by the Fourteenth Amendment, it also had to consider what rights an unborn fetus might have. The justices observed that the Constitution grants legal rights only to "persons born or naturalized in the United States." After looking at every mention of "person" in the Constitution, the justices concluded that it protects only the lives of those who are already born.

But the justices also recognized that the problem of defining exactly when life begins was a "most sensitive and difficult question." They concluded that they could not define when a fetus becomes a person. After all, they argued, physicians, philosophers, and theologians had not reached agreement on the question.

People opposed to abortion rights saw the vague stance on personhood as a fundamental weakness in the *Roe* v. *Wade* decision. In 1973 alone, several bills were introduced in Congress that defined personhood as beginning

Senator James Buckley publicly joined the abortion debate in 1973 when he proposed a "human life amendment" that would have defined "personhood" as beginning at the moment of conception. Buckley's proposal was endorsed by six other senators.

at conception. The best known of these was a "human life amendment" proposed by Republican senator James Buckley and six other senators. A version of the Buckley bill would be regularly reintroduced in the years to come.

Viability

The Supreme Court had obviously struggled with the question of personhood. Although they could not decide when life began, the justices believed that a fetus should have some protection as a "potential life." Potential life, they reasoned, begins at viability—when the fetus could survive outside the mother's womb. Viability, they said, would be decided by a qualified physician. Then the state could restrict abortion to protect a potential life.

However, critics of the decision felt that the Supreme Court gave physicians and states no real voice in the delicate issue of viability. The Court had imposed a strict trimester framework for when abortions could take place. In the first two trimesters, or first six months, physicians and the state could not interfere with a woman's decision to have an abortion unless her life or health would be endangered

The Court had based its trimester framework on when most fetuses are expected to be viable—that is, between the twenty-fourth and twenty-eighth week, or right after the sixth month of pregnancy. But fetuses had in fact been found to survive when they were born in the twenty-second week, and sometimes earlier. Also, many medical advances since 1973 made it possible to keep premature babies alive until their own lungs and other organs were strong enough to support life. That is why, as medical science becomes more sophisticated, the lines of viability become more and more blurred.

Many opponents of abortion rights believe that a fetus is "potential life" from the point of conception. The laws, they argue, should weigh the mother's rights against a fetus's right to life from the first month, not after the second trimester.

Even those who support abortion rights have sometimes objected to the trimester system. Since 1973, more and more abortion clinics and physicians are choosing to provide abortions only in the first trimester or until the middle of the second trimester.

The medical community won the legal right to refuse to perform abortions in 1974, when Congress passed a "conscience clause" bill. The conscience clause permitted any individual or hospital opposed to abortions to refuse to perform them. By 1975, about 83 percent of public hospitals and 72 percent of private, non-Catholic hospitals refused to perform abortions. This led to the widespread growth of private abortion clinics. But most abortion facilities were built in urban centers. Abortion-rights activists complained that poor women living in rural areas were hurt by the "conscience clause."

States' Rights

Individual states have traditionally maintained that their laws can better serve the beliefs of smaller communities. The U.S. government and state governments must work to maintain a delicate balance between laws that protect the many and laws that protect particular populations.

The pro-life movement has organized an annual March for Life in Washington, D.C., since the first anniversary of *Roc* v. *Wade* in 1974. The march has grown from 6,000 participants in 1974 to more than 200,000 in the early 1990s.

Many state lawmakers felt that *Roe* v. *Wade* infringed on their rights to decide what was best for their local citizens. Justice White, in his dissenting opinion, echoed this same position, by asserting: "I find no constitutional warrant for imposing such an order of priorities on the people and legislatures of the States. . . . This issue, for the most part, should be left with the people and to the political processes the people have devised to govern their affairs."

The Supreme Court decision allowed states to restrict abortion in order to protect the potential life of the fetus, unless the mother's life or health was endangered. But these restrictions could apply only after the sixth month of pregnancy. Many states acted quickly to impose new laws. In 1973, over two hundred abortion bills were introduced in state legislatures. But many of these were so restrictive that they were dismissed in court challenges.

Brewing Controversy

The debates over personhood, viability, and states' rights began in the first few years after *Roe* v. *Wade*. They accelerated into a major national issue, though, when pro-life and then pro-choice activists organized powerful, vocal lobbies and public campaigns in the late 1970s.

The first to organize were those who opposed abortion rights. Viewing the *Roe* v. *Wade* decision as a threat to their fundamental beliefs, pro-life advocates felt that they had to become politically active to "protect the sanctity of human life."

The National Right to Life Committee (NRLC), one of the most powerful pro-life groups today, formed six months after the *Roe* v. *Wade* decision came down. The group was organized like a senate, with two directors elected by local pro-life leaders in each state. Organized in this way, the NRLC could take its message into every state at a grass-roots, or local, level.

Some pro-life groups have resorted to illegal and violent methods in their attempt to restrict abortion rights in America. Here, a doctor stands over the broken glass that rained down in his examination room when his clinic was bombed by extremists.

In 1976, New York Democrat Ellen McCormack became the first person to run for president on a single-issue, pro-life platform.

Three months later, Catholic leaders also resolved to begin a grass-roots campaign to outlaw abortion. By 1975, the National Conference of Catholic Bishops— an old archenemy of abortion rights—had developed a "pastoral plan" to lobby state legislatures and the U.S. Congress. What did the bishops want? A constitutional amendment declaring abortion a criminal act.

On January 22, 1974, the first anniversary of the *Roe* v. *Wade* decision, some 6,000 pro-life demonstrators staged their first annual March for Life in Washington, D.C. More people joined the demonstrations yearly. By 1990, the March for Life had grown to include over 200,000 pro-life advocates.

In 1976, a pro-life activist ran for the highest political office in the country. Ellen McCormack, a housewife from New York, became a candidate for the Democratic presidential nomination and entered nineteen state primaries. Other politicians could not ignore the fact that she received over 267,000 votes. That was a surprisingly large number of votes for an unknown woman who ran on a single issue—restricting abortion rights.

Randall Terry heads Operation Rescue, a radical pro-life activist group that demonstrates and blocks access to abortion clinics across the country.

Abortion-Rights Politics

Ellen McCormack's minor success in the primaries showed politicians that people would vote on the abortion-rights issue alone. Both the Democratic and the Republican parties thought about including a stand on abortion rights in their election year platforms for 1976. But only the Republican party adopted a position. This was the first year that the Republican party officially opposed abortion rights in its platform.

Over the next few years, two anti-abortion groups—the National Pro-Life Political Action Committee and the Life Amendment Political Action Committee—would lobby to drive pro-choice members of Congress out of office.

Spending Public Money on Abortion

Critics of public policy on abortion—whether they support or oppose abortion—often claim that politics and abortion don't mix. Abortion, they point out, is too personal and moral an issue to be legislated fairly. The Constitution protects our right to hold differing moral beliefs, they say, but it does not spell out what is right or wrong. Critics also argue that personal beliefs about abortion are often rooted in religion. Religion, according to the Constitution, must be kept separate from the workings of government.

In reality the lines between personal beliefs and public policy are not always clearly divided. When the *Roe* v. *Wade* decision was made, Congress was anxious not to offend the portion of the population that personally opposed abortion. One way to work around the new laws was to make sure that tax dollars would not be used to support abortion.

In 1974, Congress passed legislation that prohibited the use of U.S. funds to support abortion services abroad. It also passed an amendment that prohibited legal-aid lawyers, whose services were supported by government funds, from handling abortion cases. Both laws affected poor women. Most family-planning services abroad were offered to poor women in less-developed countries. Legal-aid services helped low-income families that could not afford a private lawyer.

Meanwhile, roughly a third of all legal abortions in the United States were being publicly funded through Medicaid. Part of a national welfare program for low-income households, Medicaid served poor women. In the first three years after abortion became legalized, over 300,000 abortions were funded by Medicaid. Enraged pro-life activists lobbied to stop these Medicaid payments; they did not want their tax dollars spent on abortions.

Pro-life activists found an ally in Henry Hyde, a conservative Republican representative to Congress. Hyde was fiercely anti-abortion and believed that a human life exists from conception. He once introduced himself to pro-life activists as a "626-month fetus." His opponents charged that Hyde brought his Roman Catholic beliefs to politics. Although Hyde denied this, he openly said that religious values should be part of political debate.

In 1976, Henry Hyde introduced an amendment that banned federal funds for all abortions, except when the life of the mother was "clearly endangered." A revised version of the Hyde Amendment was passed by Congress in 1977, a year later. The amendment banned federal funding for abortions, except when the woman's life was in danger, when the pregnancy would result in "severe and long-lasting physical damage," or if the pregnancy had been caused by a reported case of rape or incest. In 1981, Congress even barred victims of rape and incest from receiving public aid.

The Hyde Amendment seemed unreasonably strict to many people, but surprisingly, both the Supreme Court and Democratic president Jimmy Carter supported it. The same year the amendment passed in Congress, the Supreme Court heard two cases, *Beal* v. *Doe* and *Maher* v.

Henry Hyde proposed an amendment in 1976 that restricted the use of federal funds for all abortions except when the life of the mother was endangered. In 1977, Congress passed a revised version of the amendment.

Roe, involving Medicaid funding for abortions. The justices declared that states could deny Medicaid funding to poor women who sought abortions unless the pregnancy was a threat to the mother's life or health. Only Justices Blackmun and Brennan., two of *Roe* v. *Wade*'s fiercest defenders, opposed the Court decision.

The Hyde Amendment and the Supreme Court decision led forty states to restrict Medicaid funding for abortions. Other legislation also banned Peace Corps volunteers and military personnel and their families from federal funding for abortions. In 1978, Congress allowed private employers to refuse to cover abortions in their employer health insurance plans.

Consent Laws

One fear raised by easy access to abortion rights was that it would encourage teenagers to become more sexually active. Missouri and Massachuetts were the first states to address this fear by requiring teenagers under eighteen to get their parents' permission before they could obtain an abortion in their state.

In *Planned Parenthood of Central Missouri* v. *Danforth* (1976) and *Bellotti* v. *Baird* (which directly challenged the Massachusetts law in 1979), the Supreme Court struck down parental consent as unconstitutional. The justices ruled that the laws violated the rights of "mature and fully competent minors." They also argued that a teenager should be able to take her case to court rather than her parents if she preferred. Other states later included the court option in their consent requirements.

The Supreme Court dismissed another kind of consent code in the Missouri laws with little argument. Missouri required married women to get their husbands' permission before they had an abortion. That law, the Court's justices declared, violated the constitutional rights outlined for women in *Roe* v. *Wade*.

The Tide Turns

Abortion rights survived the bitter debates of the 1970s. The *Roe* v. *Wade* decision sparked heated exchanges in Congress and on the streets, but it was basically respected. The decision's strength led anti-abortion groups to mobilize as forcefully as they did, sometimes even becoming violent. Radical pro-life groups had been picketing, bombing, and setting fire to abortion clinics since the mid-1970s. Physicians who performed abortions became used to death threats and hate mail. However, the majority of people lived peacefully with the new laws. Public opinion on abortion has actually changed very little since *Roe* v. *Wade* was first decided. The major difference was that women quietly sought legal abortions instead of fearfully resorting to illegal abortions.

By 1980, though, the political tide had turned against abortion rights. Opponents of abortion joined forces with a growing conservative movement in the country. The movement was sometimes called "pro-family" or the "New Right." It gained great political power in 1980, when Ronald Reagan was elected president. President Reagan was openly against abortion, and the Republican party that nominated him had already declared that it would support a human-life amendment in Congress to overturn *Roe* v. *Wade*. The party also vowed that judges who opposed abortion rights would be appointed to federal courts under the Reagan administration. For the eight years that Reagan was in the White House, the Republicans would make good on their promise. The Reagan years—and four years under George Bush that followed—would see five of the Court's nine justices replaced with conservative-oriented members. The decade of the 1980s would soon prove to be one of the most pivotal in the history of abortion. During those years, the executive branch would create one of the most significant shifts in the balance of power the Court had ever seen.

Ronald Reagan ran for president in 1980 with a strong stand against abortion rights. During his administration, the "balance of power" on the Supreme Court was profoundly changed by appointments of conservative justices who were openly sympathetic to restricting abortion laws.

Chapter 4

Abortion Today: Chipping Away at *Roe* v. *Wade*

P ro-choice activists had been quiet through the 1970s compared with pro-life groups. *Roe* v. *Wade* had given people who supported abortion rights what they wanted. But there was reason to fear that the landmark decision of 1973 would be overturned in the 1980s.

With the support of the Republican party and the White House, several members of Congress had reintroduced human-life amendments that granted personhood to a fetus from conception. These bills usually died because Congress and pro-life groups couldn't come to an agreement. But revised versions of these bills continued to surface throughout the 1980s.

As a response to the growing momentum of the pro-life movement, abortion-rights groups organized in thirty-five states during the 1980s. Like the pro-life movement, they launched a political action campaign. Their goal was to protect the rights won in 1973. In January of 1983, when pro-life demonstrators held their annual March for Life, pro-choice activists also held rallies and news conferences to mark the tenth anniversary of *Roe* v. *Wade*.

Meanwhile, militant pro-life groups were held responsible for more violent protests at abortion facilities across the country. The pro-life movement had long been supported by fundamentalist Christians and Catholic groups. Now support for its position grew in every branch of government and among conservative citizens.

Even the June 1992 decision did not lessen the debate that continues to rage across the nation.

Opposite:
Since 1973, more than eleven Supreme Court decisions have modified or limited the power of the original *Roe* v. *Wade* decision.

More Restrictions on Public Funding

Public funding for abortion became quite scarce in the 1980s. The Supreme Court supported the Hyde Amendment in a 1980 court case, *Harris* v. *McRae*. In separate cases, the Court decided that states were not required to fund abortions either. By 1981, Congress stopped the funding of abortions for low-income women who were the victims of rape or incest.

By 1989, many in the U.S. Senate thought the cuts in public funding for abortion had been too extreme. They passed a bill that allowed the District of Columbia to use its own tax dollars to fund abortions for many low-income women. The Senate also voted to resume certain Medicaid funding for abortion patients who were the victims of rape or incest. A bill to give funds to a United Nations–sponsored family planning program for other countries barely passed through the Senate.

All three bills were vetoed by President Bush. Bush had favored abortion rights before he became vice president under Reagan, but by the time he won the presidency in 1988, he had become fiercely anti-abortion.

Consent Laws and Waiting Periods

States continued to exercise their state rights by enacting new laws that limited access to abortion. Teenage pregnancy remained a concern throughout the 1980s. States responded with more parental consent laws.

Critics of abortion rights were also concerned that women of all ages might take abortion too lightly. Two kinds of laws that answered this concern were requirements for "waiting periods" and an "informed consent clause." A mandatory waiting period meant that a woman would have to put off an abortion for a certain amount of time—twenty-four or forty-eight hours—after she first tried to obtain it. The extra time, lawmakers argued, would give her a chance to weigh her decision. Informed consent laws required abortion providers to tell patients about fetal development, the psychological and physical risks of abortion, and alternatives to abortion.

Strong New Challenges

In 1989, the Supreme Court heard the most serious challenge yet to *Roe* v. *Wade*. The justices had already decided seven major court cases during the decade of the 1980s and had made many concessions to the pro-life movement that was rapidly gaining power. Concessions the justices made led pro-life groups to hope that the Supreme Court itself might actually overturn *Roe* v. *Wade* in the near future. The new Supreme Court case that opponents of abortion rights hoped would challenge *Roe* v. *Wade* involved a new set of Missouri laws. The case, *Webster* v. *Reproductive Health Services*, worried those who supported abortion rights as much as it inspired hope in people who were pro-life. What was so different about this lawsuit?

Webster v. *Reproductive Health Services*

For the first time, a state statute was openly challenging the *Roe* v. *Wade* decision. The preamble, or introduction, to the Missouri abortion laws stated that the "life of each human being begins at conception" and that unborn children should be given "all the rights, privileges, and immunities available to other persons, citizens, and residents of the state." Lawyers for Missouri claimed that the statement was just an introduction and not meant to be enforced. Reproductive Health Services argued that the preamble would effectively cause physicians and clinics to stop performing abortions.

While Missouri's lawyers denied that the preamble would restrict abortion rights, they also requested the Supreme Court to make a dramatic decision in connection with the Missouri case. They recommended that the

Court overturn *Roe* v. *Wade*. This recommendation caused heated debate among the justices and was of great concern to pro-choice factions everywhere.

Changed Times

As the Supreme Court deliberated on *Webster* v. *Reproductive Health Services*, people opposed to *Roe* v. *Wade* had good reason to be hopeful that the decision would come down in their favor. The Reagan and Bush administrations had helped to foster anti-abortion legislation. More important, though, was the way the Republican presidents had affected federal courts in the 1980s. As the Republican party had promised, the new judges were appointed as much for their stands against abortion as for any other qualifications.

Only three of the original drafters of the *Roe* v. *Wade* decision still remained on the Supreme Court in 1989. William O. Douglas, one of the original seven supporters of *Roe* v. *Wade,* had already retired in 1975. (He was replaced by the conservative justice John Paul Stevens. Stevens, though, favored legal abortion.) Justice Potter Stewart, who had voted for *Roe* v. *Wade*, retired in 1981. Chief Justice Warren Burger retired in 1986. Although Justice Burger had been a conservative, he had also voted with the 7-2 majority in *Roe* v. *Wade*. Lewis F. Powell, another justice who had voted for abortion rights in 1973, retired in 1987.

President Reagan replaced the retiring justices with Sandra Day O'Connor, Antonin Scalia, and Anthony Kennedy. All three had conservative records, although it was unclear whether they would vote for or against abortion rights. Reagan also appointed William Rehnquist as chief justice. Rehnquist had opposed the *Roe* v. *Wade* decision and was fiercely anti-abortion. Byron White, the only other justice who had opposed the 1973 decision, was still sitting on the Court in 1989.

Mixed Opinions

Waiting for the Court's decision in *Webster* v. *Reproductive Health Services*, both pro-life and pro-choice activists stepped up their campaigns. In April 1989, each side staged a massive rally in Washington to sway the Court's decision. The decision that came down two months later, however, worried those on both sides of the issue.

The Supreme Court declared several Missouri statutes to be legal in the *Webster* case of 1989. The state, the Court said, could prohibit the use of public facilities and employees for abortion. It could require physicians to test fetuses for viability after the twentieth week of gestation. It could ban state funds for "encouraging and counseling women on the abortion procedure." (Known popularly as the "gag rule," this aspect of the decision cut down on public access to abortion information and counseling.) None of these concessions were especially dramatic, given the Court's record in the 1980s. Why, then, were people who supported abortion rights so worried?

Part of a Supreme Court ruling in 1989 allowed states to restrict the use of federal funds for abortion counseling. Pro-choice advocates labeled this provision the "gag rule" because they felt it was a dangerous form of state censorship.

What was most significant about the *Webster* case was what some of the justices said about *Roe* v. *Wade*. Justice Rehnquist attacked the trimester framework set up by *Roe* v. *Wade*, pointing out that it was not up to the Court to decide when a fetus becomes viable. The trimester system, he said, had led to "a web of legal rules that have become increasingly intricate." Rehnquist also stated that he believed the *Roe* v. *Wade* decision was wrong in limiting states' rights to protect the fetus until it was viable.

Justice Scalia was more outspoken against the 1973 decision. He claimed that *Roe* v. *Wade* should have been on trial instead of the Missouri statutes. Scalia predicted, "We can now look forward to at least another term with carts full of mail from the public, and streets full of demonstrators, urging us . . . to follow the popular will."

Justice Blackmun, the author of the *Roe* v. *Wade* decision, remained loyal to his original position. He warned: "Today, *Roe* v. *Wade*, and the fundamental constitutional right of women to decide whether to terminate a pregnancy, survive but are not secure. . . . I fear for the future. I fear for the liberty and equality of the millions of women who have lived and come of age in the sixteen years since *Roe* was decided."

Backlash

The Supreme Court traditionally unifies the public on controversial issues. But the justices were bitterly divided on the issue of abortion rights. The *Webster* case caused a flurry of activity both for and against abortion rights.

A bill for the Freedom of Choice Act was introduced to Congress in 1991. Its supporters hoped that it would help bolster the now-fragile *Roe* v. *Wade* decision. The act would forbid states from restricting abortion "before fetal viability" and at any time when the woman's life or health was in danger. The bill had strong support in both houses, but its fate was unclear.

Colorado representative Pat Schroeder was one of the key supporters of the Freedom of Choice Act, introduced to Congress in 1991. The bill aimed to reinforce many of the rights and freedoms granted by *Roe* v. *Wade*.

Pro-choice activists staged an angry demonstration in Washington in response to the *Webster* decision. Again, hundreds of thousands of people gathered to protest the weakening policies on abortion rights. Meanwhile, pro-life activists continued to try to shut down abortion clinics and "save unborn lives."

The territory of Guam and the states of Idaho, Utah, Pennsylvania, and Louisiana passed laws that prohibited abortion in most cases. Utah's laws were so strict that abortion-rights supporters recommended a boycott of Utah tourism.

Amid this already divisive climate, the Supreme Court began deliberating on another major abortion case, *Planned Parenthood of Southeastern Pennsylvania* v. *Casey.* Supporters on both sides of the issue were sure that this time the reach and power of *Roe* v. *Wade* would be significantly changed and firmly decided.

The Pennsylvania Challenge

The Pennsylvania Abortion Control Act of 1989 was one of the strictest abortion laws in the country. When it reached the Supreme Court in 1992, lawyers arguing for Pennsylvania's laws also attached a formal request that the Supreme Court overturn *Roe* v. *Wade.* The potential significance of this case alarmed many pro-choice advocates. On April 5, just two weeks before the case was to be heard, one of the largest demonstrations in history took place in front of the Capitol to protest the possible erosion of *Roe* v. *Wade.* The justices deliberated until June 29, 1992. Again, pro-life and pro-choice activists rallied and campaigned for their sides up to the last minute.

The Supreme Court's June 1992 decision, in a 5-4 ruling, declared most of Pennsylvania's strict laws constitutional. These legal laws included:

- A mandatory twenty-four hour waiting period before an abortion could be performed.

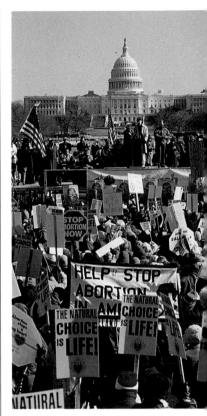

By the late 1980s and early 1990s, the pro-life movement had consolidated a great deal of support. Well-organized lobbies in Washington and the staging of high-profile media events did much to draw national attention to the pro-life cause.

The Abortion Pill Controversy

RU 486, a pill that causes abortion, has been the subject of much controversy. Manufactured by a French pharmaceutical firm, Roussel Uclaf, the pill is available by prescription only in France and a handful of other countries. It is taken in the presence of a physician. The abortion occurs at home within forty-eight hours.

RU 486 is effective only in the first eight weeks of pregnancy. Some women have reported serious side effects from RU 486, such as severe bleeding. But the drug is also regarded as a medical breakthrough: It can replace more costly surgical procedures in an early abortion. The drug's supporters claim that it is safer than surgery. It is also of interest to researchers who are seeking new treatments for breast cancer, Alzheimer's disease, and kidney failure. But RU 486 was banned in the United States.

The abortion pill became a part of the political debate over abortion when the Food and Drug Administration (FDA) put an "import alert" on the drug, refusing to let it into the United States even for testing and research. Abortion-rights activists claim that the FDA responded to pressure from abortion opponents.

Anti-abortion groups have strongly opposed the abortion pill and declared that they will protest the sale of RU 486 in the United States. Meanwhile, pro-choice groups argue that the drug would benefit women who cannot withstand the anesthetics used in surgical abortion procedures. They also point out that a drug in pill form would encourage women to seek early abortions.

The FDA ban against RU 486 was challenged before the Supreme Court in July 1992. The case involved an unmarried woman from California, Leona Benten, who had volunteered as a "test case" for an activist group called Abortion Rights Mobilization to travel to England for twelve RU 486 pills. The pills were prescribed to end her six-week pregnancy but were confiscated by U.S. customs officials.

The Supreme Court refused Benten's request that the abortion pills be returned to her, on the grounds that she could not prove that the FDA ban had been imposed illegally. The case may be heard again, but in a lower court.

Eleanor Smeal, president of NOW, displays a pile of petitions supporting the legalization of RU 486.

- An "informed consent" clause that required abortion providers to give abortion patients state-prepared information about abortion and fetal development.
- Parental or judicial consent before a minor could have an abortion.

The court struck down a law that would have required a woman to get her husband's consent before an abortion. In making this decision, Justice O'Connor introduced a new way to measure whether an abortion law violated a woman's constitutional rights. She applied an "undue burden" analysis, explaining that an "undue burden exists, and therefore a provision of law is invalid, if its purpose or effect is to place a substantial obstacle in the path of a woman seeking an abortion before the fetus attains viability." Critics complained that "undue burden" was too vague a term. They predicted that it would lead to still more complicated court battles.

What the public and lawmakers had waited for, however, was not the decision on a specific state's laws. Everyone had wondered if the Supreme Court would, in fact, overturn *Roe* v. *Wade*.

Roe v. *Wade* Affirmed

In their joint 184-page opinion, Justices O'Connor, Kennedy, and Souter stated: "After considering the fundamental constitutional questions resolved by Roe . . . we are led to conclude this: the essential holding of *Roe* v. *Wade* should be retained and once again reaffirmed." The Court's statement was far less critical of the 1973 decision than it had been when the justices decided *Webster*.

But critics of the Pennsylvania decision believed that it had eroded many of the rights established by *Roe* v. *Wade*. After all, most of the Pennsylvania law had been upheld. Also, the Court declared that it did not like the trimester system set up in *Roe* v. *Wade*. Together with the new "undue burden" clause, pro-choice advocates argued, these decisions would lead the Court to "chip away" at *Roe* v. *Wade* until little of it was left.

Justice Blackmun feared that the one "swing vote" that had saved *Roe* v. *Wade* in *Planned Parenthood of Southeastern Pennsyvania* v. *Casey* could easily go the other way the next time the 1973 decision was threatened. He was the last remaining justice from the 1973 Supreme Court who had voted for *Roe* v. *Wade*. (Justice Thurgood Marshall retired in 1991 and was replaced by the more conservative Clarence Thomas.) Blackmun's fears were reinforced by the conservative dissenting opinion of his colleague

The 1992 Supreme Court posed for a formal portrait only months before the Pennsylvania case was heard. Back row (left to right): David Souter, Antonin Scalia, Anthony Kennedy, and Clarence Thomas. Front row (left to right): John Paul Stevens, Byron White, Chief Justice William Rehnquist, Harry Blackmun, and Sandra Day O'Connor.

Antonin Scalia. Justice Scalia wrote: "The central issue of the case is not whether the power of a woman to abort her unborn child is liberty in the absolute sense; or even whether it is a liberty of great importance to many women. Of course, it is both. The issue is whether it is a liberty protected by the Constitution of the United States. I am sure that it is not."

Mixed Feelings

The final ruling of the Court in the Pennsylvania case seemed not to carry the ground-breaking impact that had been anticipated for so long. This was partly because the ruling was ultimately decided by a new "moderate middle" (O'Connor, Kennedy, and Souter) that was expected to offer more conservative opinions but, in fact, came down squarely in "the middle" on the issue. Without a clear pro-life or pro-choice outcome, neither side on the abortion debate was pleased with the Pennsylvania decision. Kate Michelman, president of the National Abortion Rights Action League, declared, "Don't be fooled by the Court's smoke screen. . . . What the Court did today is devastating for women."

Meanwhile, Randall Terry, the leader of Operation Rescue, said "three Reagan-Bush appointees stabbed the pro-life movement in the back" when they clearly upheld *Roe* v. *Wade*.

The Political "Hot Potato"

The nationwide debate on abortion that continued through the summer of 1992 soon became an integral part of the presidential campaign that was under way. As it had been since the 1970s, abortion was an important issue for both candidates to address. Democratic candidate Bill Clinton was openly pro-choice and, in fact, said that he would be the "pro-choice president." With the Democratic party's official backing, Clinton made abortion rights a central issue in his campaign.

George Bush, in contrast to his opponent, did not have a clear mandate from his party colleagues. The abortion debate heated up again in August 1992, as the Republican party deliberated on its convention platform.

Abortion rights became a central issue in the 1992 presidential campaign. Democratic candidate Bill Clinton strongly supported freedom of choice and vowed to be the first "pro-choice president."

After *Roe* v. *Wade:*
The Landmark Cases

Roe v. *Wade* sparked a national debate over abortion rights that has continued to this day. In 1973, some said the decision was "too liberal" and left abortion too free and uncontrolled. Others realized that the case did not, in fact, erase all limitations or restrictions on abortion. After all, states could still regulate abortions during the middle and last trimesters of pregnancy.

Over the past nineteen years, additional Supreme Court decisions have modified and constricted the rights outlined in *Roe* v. *Wade*. The following is a listing of some of those key decisions.

1976 *Planned Parenthood* v. *Danforth*

The Court voted 6-3 that a husband's consent is not required to obtain an abortion and that parents cannot prevent a minor daughter from having an abortion.

1977 *Maher* v. *Roe*

The Court voted 6-3 that states may refuse to spend public funds (meaning Medicaid) to provide "nontherapeutic" abortions for poor women.

1979 *Colautti* v. *Franklin*

The Court voted 6-3 that states may seek to protect a fetus that a physician has determined could survive outside the womb.

1979 *Belloti* v. *Baird*

The Court voted 8-1 that a state cannot require pregnant unmarried minors to get parental consent for an abortion. The ruling said parental consent violated the rights of "mature" and "competent" minors.

1980 *Harris* v. *McRae*

The Court voted 5-4 to uphold the Hyde Amendment, which denies federal reimbursement for Medicaid abortions.

1981 *H.L.* v. *Matheson*

The Court voted 6-3 that states may require a doctor to notify the parents before a minor undergoes an abortion.

1983 *City of Akron* v. *Akron Center for Reproductive Health*

The Court voted 6-3 that states cannot mandate what doctors tell abortion patients or require that abortions for women more than three months pregnant be performed in a hospital.

1986 *Thornburgh* v. *American College of Obstetricians and Gynecologists*

The Court voted 5-4 that states may require physicians to tell women about the risks of abortion or about alternatives.

1989 *Webster* v. *Reproductive Health Services*

The Court upheld 5-4 Missouri's law barring the use of public facilities or public employees in performing abortions. The Court also upheld the states' right to require physicians to determine the fetus's viability if the fetus was believed to be more than twenty weeks old.

1991 *Rust* v. *Sullivan*

The Court upheld 5-4 the federal government's ban on abortion counseling in federally funded family-planning clinics.

1992 *Planned Parenthood of Southeastern Pennsylvania* v. *Casey*

The Court upheld the constitutionality of *Roe* v. *Wade* and voted down mandatory notification of husbands. The Court did uphold mandatory waiting periods of twenty-four hours before an abortion could proceed.

Since 1980, the Republicans had not shied away from taking an openly tough stance against abortion rights. In addition, they had advertised their determination to appoint only pro-life jurists to the Supreme Court. But anticipation of a strong anti-*Roe* decision in the Pennsylvania case had done much to scare noncommitted or inactive pro-choice sympathizers into strengthening their forces. Some of these newly invigorated pro-choice people were members of the Republican party, even those who were quite conservative on most other issues. The call from many of these Republicans was for a moderate stand on abortion or—at the very least—no specific stand in the official platform at all.

Although strong pro-choice voices in the party threatened an embarrassing protest and debate on the floor of the Houston convention, Republican pro-life powers retained their hold on the party's platform. Not only did the party openly oppose abortion rights, it also called for a constitutional amendment to ban all abortions.

What Next?

Will the Supreme Court overturn *Roe* v. *Wade* in the future? The Court takes its precedents seriously, but it has also overturned over a hundred earlier decisions in the course of its history. If *Roe* v. *Wade* were overturned, would abortion be illegal nationwide? Most probably not. States would make their own laws, and recent history shows that most states would allow abortion under at least some circumstances.

Since 1973, states have tried to strike a compromise between the two extreme views that say abortion is a criminal act or that women should have unrestricted access to abortion. The most common state laws have restricted abortion with consent requirements, informed consent, parental or spousal notification, and waiting periods. Other laws include restrictions on abortion funding and on abortion clinics. Concerns about early viability have led some states to set earlier cut-off dates for legal abortions. Finally, some states have wanted to restrict the allowable reasons for an abortion.

What Does the Public Think?

Public-opinion polls are often criticized as unreliable because people answer questions differently depending on how they are asked. For example, more people have been

During his administration, President Bush was strongly in favor of restricting abortion rights. During his bid for reelection in 1992, both he and the Republican party put forth a platform advocating a constitutional amendment that would once again make abortion illegal in America.

A prolonged and intense demonstration by pro-life activists in Wichita, Kansas, in 1991 went on for more than three months. By continuously blocking entrances to abortion clinics and denying women access to care, this demonstration sparked new debates over the legality and limitations of protest in America.

found to favor abortion rights if the question includes the phrase "woman's right to choose" than if it refers to "protecting an unborn child."

A 1990 Harris poll showed that 73 percent of the public favored "giving a woman, with the advice of her physician, the right to choose to have an abortion." In *New York Times*/CBS polls, 62 percent have consistently favored abortion rights. But only 46 percent say abortion should be as unrestricted as it is now.

Polls show that many Americans can live with abortion rights even if they personally object to abortion. The same person who agrees that abortion is morally wrong will often also support the legal right to abortion. The public is most likely to support abortion rights for a health or life risk to the mother, fetal defects, incest, and rape. A clear majority of Americans feel that abortion is not always justified for unwed mothers or if the mother can't afford to have a baby.

Pending Cases

Several abortion cases had been pending in district courts when the Supreme Court was deliberating on the Pennsylvania laws in 1991 and 1992. Three of these cases became invalid after the Court issued its decision in June 1992. These cases challenged new abortion laws in Guam, Louisiana, and Utah. Guam had banned almost all abortions. Louisiana had banned all abortions except those performed to save the woman's life and if the pregnancy resulted from reported rape or incest. Utah's law was similar to Louisiana's. But Utah also permitted abortion for serious fetal deformities. In addition, Utah would permit abortions for rape or incest only before twenty weeks of gestation.

Less strict laws were also being challenged. *Fargo Women's Health Organization* v. *Sinner* challenged a 1991 North Dakota law that required informed consent and a twenty-four hour waiting period. *Barnes* v. *Moore* challenged a Mississippi law requiring informed consent and a seventy-two hour waiting period. Both laws were under injunction blocking their enforcement in 1991, pending a court decision. Another case, *Coe* v. *Melahn*, involved a ban on private health insurance for abortion. As of September 1992, the case was continuing. The Court's ruling in the Pennsylvania case would undoubtedly serve as a precedent in all three of these cases.

The Debate Continues

Meanwhile, in the aftermath of the Pennsylvania decision, the debate on abortion continued. Operation Rescue blockaded clinics across the country, even though there was a Supreme Court case—*Bray* v. *Alexandria Women's Health Clinic*—pending against the organization's right to do so. Instead of settling issues on either side of the abortion debate, the Pennsylvania case seemed only to strengthen the resolve of both sides. Both pro-life and pro-choice activists stepped up their media campaigns after the Pennsylvania case was decided.

Justice Harry Blackmun, in his opinion on the Pennsylvania case, warned that lines in the abortion fight may be redrawn in the near future. Blackmun wrote, "I am eighty-three years old. I cannot remain on this Court forever and when I do step down, the confirmation process for my successor well may focus on the issue before us today. That, I regret, may be exactly where the choice between the two worlds will be made."

Both pro-life and pro-choice factions had anticipated a great deal of significance in the Pennsylvania ruling. And, though the case was a landmark for the legal status of abortion in America, it did not "satisfy" or silence advocates on any side. The Pennsylvania case simply proved, as most cases are likely to prove in decades to come, that the abortion debate may never be permanently silenced.

Chronology

1821	The first laws to limit abortion are passed in Connecticut.	**January 22, 1973**	The Supreme Court declares Texas abortion laws unconstitutional with *Roe* v. *Wade*.
1959	The American Law Institute proposes legalized abortion if the pregnancy is likely to "impair the physical or mental health of the mother." Within ten years, fourteen states had passed laws modeled on the proposal.	**January 22, 1974**	The first annual pro-life demonstration, March for Life, is held in Washington, D.C.
1962	In Arizona, Shari Finkbine seeks to abort a fetus that is thought to be deformed. She is forced to go to Sweden.	**1974**	Congress passes a "conscience clause" law allowing hospitals to refuse to perform abortions, leading to the growth of private clinics.
1967	The American Medical Association declares itself in favor of more liberal abortion laws.	**1977**	The Hyde Amendment, banning federally funded abortions, is passed by Congress.
1969	The Supreme Court overturns Washington, D.C., abortion laws as vague.	**1989**	The Supreme Court upholds Missouri state laws prohibiting the use of public facilities for abortions.
May 22, 1970	The *Roe* v. *Wade* "class-action" suit is filed in a Texas court, contending that women have a constitutional right to choose abortion.	**June 29, 1992**	The Supreme Court upholds *Roe* v. *Wade* while declaring strict Pennsylvania laws constitutional.

For Further Reading

Friedman, Leon, ed. *The Justices of the United States Supreme Court.* Broomall, PA: Chelsea House, 1991.

Schlesinger, Arthur M., Jr., ed. *The Supreme Court.* Broomall. PA: Chelsea House, 1989.

Simpson, Carolyn. *Coping with an Unplanned Pregnancy.* New York: Rosen Publishing, 1990.

Summer, Lila, and Woods, Samuel G. *The Judiciary.* Austin, TX: Raintree Steck-Vaughn, 1992.

Wharton, Mandy. *Abortion.* New York: Franklin Watts, 1989.

Wharton, Mandy. *Rights of Women.* New York: Franklin Watts, 1989.

Index

Acknowledgments and Photo Credits

Cover: Blackbirch Graphics, Inc.; p. 4: © Luc Novovitch/Gamma-Liaison; pp. 7, 20, 21, 32, 34, 36, 37, 39, 41, 43, 46, 51, 52, 53, 54, 56, 59, 60: Wide World Photos; pp. 9, 57: © Brad Markel/Gamma-Liaison; p. 11: © Joe Traver/Gamma-Liaison; p. 12: North Wind Photo Archives; p. 14: © Sandra Baker/Liaison International; p.16: © Michael Springer/Gamma-Liaison; p. 25: © Bruce Glassman; p. 28: © Fame/Gamma-Liaison; p. 30: Associated Press; p. 40: © John Chiasson/Gamma-Liaison; p. 42: © Michael Okoniewski/Gamma-Liaison; p. 45: The White House.